An Epidemic of Joy

Stories in the Spirit of Jesus

Andrew M. Greeley

Mary Greeley Durkin

ACTA
PUBLICATIONS

An Epidemic of Joy
Stories in the Spirit of Jesus
by Andrew M. Greeley and Mary Greeley Durkin

Edited by Gregory F. Augustine Pierce
Cover design by Tom A. Wright
Text design and typesetting by Garrison Publications

Published by ACTA Publications,
Assisting Christians To Act, 4848 N. Clark Street,
Chicago, IL 60640, 800-397-2282.

Library of Congress Catalog Number: 98-74567

ISBN: 0-87946-194-2

Printed in the United States of America

03 02 01 00 99 5 4 3 2 1 First Printing

Contents

Foreword

If you like bite-size stories, cameos, snapshots, vignettes, you have picked up the right book.

If you do not like your meanings prepackaged and served to you with all the messiness eliminated, you have picked up the right book.

If you like to be teased and provoked into thinking, you have picked up the right book.

If you like to imagine gospel stories and sayings as a tightly wound ball of yarn that can be pulled out to full beauty, you have picked up the right book.

Brother and sister storytellers Andrew Greeley and Mary Durkin have selected familiar gospel passages and then told short stories of daily life. The key for the reader is to make the connection between the gospel and the narrative. The authors, true to strict storytelling code, do not provide it. The meaning, as they say, is the reader's contribution.

There is no way to summarize the themes of this rich volume. But if a wag would refuse my reluctance and say, "Oh, try," I would suggest this: grace is always present, but we seldom see it coming.

In the ordinary flow of events, however, something pushes us into hidden mystery, and we are invited to both wisdom and repentance. Neither are cheap. The wisdom has to be reached for, and the repentance has to be worked at. The people of Greeley and Durkin's parables are always close to loving energies and display both cleverness at deflecting those energies and eagerness in receiving them.

- A self-righteous adult car driver is forgiven by a new, teenage car driver.
- A woman works at a wedding dress with hidden motives.
- A wife and mother insists on a feast for her reluctant family.
- A young boy hoards marbles and trips on the road to salvation.
- A contemporary Paschal has a near-death experience and figures out the odds.
- A young woman awakens to the music of "Scarlet Ribbons" and finally finds peace in her father's passing.
- A "candy striper" becomes a caring shepherd at the birth of a female Christ.

I think you will puzzle these people and come to the conclusion that the real target of Greeley and Durkin's storytelling is you, the reader. The upshot is that although this book is divided into short sections it is not a quick read. You will put it down again and again to ponder and assess. What is going on here? And when and if the stories hit home, what is going on in you?

F. Scott Fitzgerald once remarked, "Pull your chair up to the edge of the precipice and let me tell you a story." No matter where you are sitting when you read these stories, when you finish some of them you will be on the edge of a precipice—a place of dangerous heights. You will be called by many of these tales to wake up and change.

I imagine this book will be a superb resource for teachers and preachers of the Christian faith. You will probably be hearing some of these stories from pulpits and in classrooms. But the wisdom that emerges from reading them should not be left solely in the hands of others. Sample—and interpret—for yourself.

Some people have lamented that there is a lack of good contemporary spiritual reading. Perhaps the more trenchant observation is that the form of spiritual reading has changed. Evocative stories have replaced tedious and often excessively pious exhortation. These stories are told in the spirit of Jesus and will put you in touch with that spirit. The rest is up to you.

John Shea
Chicago, Illinois

Introduction

Stories are the way humans explain life (and themselves) to others (and to themselves). They are the natural method of human expression.

When the little kids beg, "Mommy, tell me a story," they are asking for mother to provide an explanation of what the overwhelming world all around them means.

Some experts think that the ability to explain a new event in terms of a previous event emerged in the human condition even before language. Others say that the true measure of human intelligence is the number and the quality of stories in a person's repertory.

Human beings have to learn to speak nonfiction. We are born with the ability to tell stories. Only when we arrive at school do people try to teach us other forms of knowledge and expression. They tell us that prose is better than poetry and nonfiction better than fiction. Yet outside of the classroom (even if we are scholars with Ph.Ds), we still tell stories when we truly want to communicate.

Recently a theologian at the University of Notre Dame wrote a book in which she attacked story homilies as a fad. Too bad for Jesus, whose normal mode of teaching was the story! Indeed, people followed him in great part because they loved his stories, especially those in which he put a new—almost an O. Henry-like—twist on a story they already knew. (For example, in the story of the vineyard owner who paid the workers who came at the eleventh hour a full day's wage, Jesus' audience knew the story as one emphasizing the industriousness of the late-starting workers. In Jesus' retelling of the story, the point was the crazy generosity of the vineyard owner. God is like that, Jesus insisted.)

In this book, we present 70 stories that we have used in homilies. In our view, the stories are not a come-on to catch the attention of a congregation so that the homilist can then drive home a nonfiction point. We believe that such a use of stories actually perverts them. Jesus did not explain his parables. The explanations we have in the gospels were probably added on by the gospel writers to explain "what Jesus meant." If Jesus wanted to teach that way, however, he would not have told stories.

Theologian and storyteller John Shea has said that the purpose of a story is not to educate or indoctrinate but to illuminate. The storyteller invites an audience into the world of the story to provide them with a new vision of the possibilities in their lives, so that they will go back to the world beyond the story with altered perceptions about life.

Stories are supposed to shake up, to challenge, and especially to illumine.

Stories lurk in people's minds and imaginations to trouble them and to comfort them. That was the purpose of Jesus when he told stories. That is the purpose of every storyteller. When people ask us what a story means, we always turn the question back on them. Usually they have pretty good answers, but they want to be assured that their answers are "right." By definition, they are!

We avoid autobiographical stories because they are too easy too tell and usually—as teenagers would be the first ones to tell us—"like, totally boring" to those who have to listen to them. (Most congregations tire quickly of stories about how wise a homilist's father or mother was!)

Many of our stories correlate with the stories of Jesus. They are not attempts to retell his stories but rather stories told "in his spirit." (Indexes are provided in the back of the book to the Gospel quotations that inspired our stories and the Sundays and Feast Days of the Liturgical Cycle on which they are read.)

These are attempts to make someone who hears one of our stories pay attention once again to a story of Jesus—as if they were hearing it for the first time. Thus our story, The Terrible Twins (see page 132), correlates with Jesus' story, The Prodigal Son (or, as we would have it, The Indulgent Father). The mother in our story has spoiled her twins rotten. The more she loves them, the worse they are. And the worse they are, the more she loves them. So does God love us. If we were writing the story over, we might have the mother say at the end, "I'm sure they'll grow up to be wonderful young women and fine mothers." God, we would argue along with Jesus, loves us into being good.

Some folks have suggested that our stories are cynical. The word they probably are looking for is "ironic." We respond that if they don't see irony in the stories of Jesus, then they have heard them much too often and need a fresh, new look—one free from moralizing and sentimentalizing. That is exactly what we have tried to do with these 70 stories.

Our stories are obviously not as good as the stories of Jesus. Whose are? But we are about the same task that he was—to comfort and to challenge.

We provide merely the sketch of a story. Each of them can be spun out with details to the storyteller's heart's desire. They can last two minutes or half an hour (or, if the storyteller is a *seanchaí,* all night). Our intention is not to present a canned story that can be retold verbatim but a skeleton of a story that will provide an opportunity for the natural storytelling ability that everyone possesses to come out.

So, welcome to the world of stories, a world Jesus knew well.

The Stories

Note to our readers: Those stories written by Andrew Greeley are followed by (AG), those by Mary Durkin by (MD).

An Epidemic of Joy

When the wine gave out, the mother of Jesus said to him, "They have no wine." And Jesus said to her, "Woman, what concern is that to you and to me? My hour has not yet come." His mother said to the servants, "Do whatever he tells you."

John 2:3-5

Once upon a time, a young woman named Grace invited 350 guests to her wedding. Her brother, Noble, said that he couldn't think of thirty-five people he could invite to his wedding, but Grace said that she had a lot more friends than he did.

Secretly, however, Grace hoped and prayed that no more than 200 of her invitees would be able to come. Alas, she had underestimated her popularity. There were more than 300 acceptances!

Grace wasn't worried so much about the caterer, she just upped the number of plates she ordered. But there was not enough room in the parish hall for that many guests, to say nothing of the orchestra and the dance floor.

At Cana, Jesus had turned water into wine, but who could enlarge overnight the size of a parish hall?

Grace's family went into panic. So did the groom's family. So did the groom. And, to tell the truth, so did the bride. But not for long.

"We'll not worry about it," Grace informed everyone. "If we ignore the problem and have a good time at the party, so will everyone else. Panic is contagious, but so is joy. So let's have an epidemic of joy. Then nothing can possibly go wrong."

Wherever there is joy, Jesus is there too— even if you can't see him.

(AG)

Babushka

> On entering the house, they saw the child with Mary his mother; and they knelt down and paid him homage. Then, opening their treasure chests, they offered him gifts of gold, frankincense, and myrrh.
>
> *Matthew 2:11*

Once upon a time, there lived in Bethlehem a woman named Babushka. She kept the cleanest and neatest house in town, and she was also the best cook.

One day, Babushka heard rumors that three kings had come to town across the desert, but she paid no attention to them because she had so much work to do. Suddenly, she heard the sounds of drums and pipes and saw a cavalcade of riders. She looked out the window, and there were three richly dressed kings coming toward her house. They told her that they had come to honor the little prince who had been born in Bethlehem, and they requested food and lodging.

So Babushka cooked a wonderful meal for them, remade all their beds, and wore herself out. The next morning the kings begged her to come with them so she too might see the little prince. Babushka said she would follow after them as soon as she finished the dishes. She cleaned the house again and then took out of a cabinet the toys of her own little prince—her baby boy who had died so long ago. She realized that she had no more need of them and decided to give them to the new little prince.

Babushka put the toys in a basket and sat down for a moment's rest before following the kings. Hours later, she woke up, grabbed the basket, and rushed into town. But they were gone and so was the little prince and his parents.

Ever since, it is said, Babushka has followed after the family. Whenever she finds a new baby, she looks to see if it is a little prince or princess. Then Babushka leaves a toy for the child.

We should all learn from Babushka's lesson: never let the important interfere with the essential.

(AG)

Back from the Dead

> Then the other disciple, who reached the tomb first, also went in, and he saw and believed; for as yet they did not understand the scripture, that he must rise from the dead.
>
> *John 20:8-9*

Once upon a time, a young man named Ned (often called Neddie by his mother and sisters) went away to college. His parents and sisters and little brother all thought that Ned was sweet, as did most of the young women in his neighborhood. Even the parish priest said that he wasn't all that bad for a teenager.

But Ned wanted to be free from the limitations his neighborhood imposed on him. He wanted to get away from his family and friends and parish. He wanted to test himself on his own, to find out what life was like when he was no longer labeled a "nice boy" or, worse, a "sweet boy." So he chose a college far away from home, all the way across the country. He couldn't come home on weekends or even at Thanksgiving.

Everyone in the parish missed Ned—his

parents and his brother and sisters especially. The house wasn't the same when Ned wasn't there.

The young women in the parish missed him, too. They missed his jokes and his smile and his deep blue eyes. Even the parish priest said the neighborhood was too quiet. They all began to think that Ned would actually like the strange place he had gone and that they never would see him again.

Finally, Ned came home for the holidays. His family (and a few of the young women in the neighborhood) met him at the airport and cheered him when he got off the plane. He hugged them all and laughed and maybe even shed a few tears. He'd never go that far away again, he promised. He loved his family and friends too much. Next year he'd transfer to a school much closer to home.

No wonder Jesus rose from the dead.

(AG)

Birthday Girl

"Then (the king) said to his slaves, 'The wedding is ready, but those invited were not worthy. Go therefore into the main streets, and invite everyone you find to the wedding banquet.'"

Matthew 22:8-9

Once upon a time, a little girl named Clare was about to have her seventh birthday party. Clare was really a birthday freak. She loved birthday parties more than any other girl her age, especially when it was for her!

Clare invited every little girl in the second grade to the party. All of them knew how generous Clare was at other people's parties, so they were certain that hers would be perfectly splendid. In fact, some even said that the goody bags Clare would give her guests would be better than the presents they would give her.

Her parents bought videotapes and cookies and cake and ice cream and some very special prizes for everyone who was coming.

But some of the girls (the most popular ones, of course) were unhappy that Clare had invited everyone—even the nerds. "What fun will a party be if the nerds are there?" they all said.

So first the popular girls made up excuses for not coming. Then some of the nerds (who didn't want anyone to think that they were nerds) said that they couldn't come either. Finally, most of the other girls decided that since nobody was going to Clare's party, they wouldn't either.

On the day of the party, only four little girls (Clare's real friends) showed up. What would they do with all the food and the games and the prizes, thought Clare's parents, who were heartbroken for their daughter.

But the birthday girl saw a bunch of boys she knew hanging around the park across the street from her house, so she invited them all in. The boys were very well behaved and hardly broke anything. Besides, they helped clean up afterward.

It was a great party after all.

(AG)

Blessed Are Those Who Laugh

Then (Jesus) looked up at his disciples and said:
> "Blessed are you who are poor,
>> for yours is the kingdom of God.
>
> "Blessed are you who are hungry now,
>> for you will be filled.
>
> "Blessed are you who weep now,
>> for you will laugh."

Luke 6:20-21

Once upon a time, there was a man who was very angry at God. One bitter cold winter, the pipes in his house froze, the motor block on his car cracked, the TV antenna fell off his roof, a tree tumbled on his garage, and everyone in his family was sick all winter long. One of his children would bring home a bug from school, it would spread to the other kids, then to his wife, and then to him. Everyone in his family was miserable and ornery.

The man's snowplow broke, and he wrenched his back shoveling snow by hand. The dog ran away, and they searched all day for him. They couldn't find him, and everyone's cold got worse. The dog, of course, came back miserable and ornery because he was so cold.

Finally, the man got marooned for three days in a snowstorm at O'Hare International Airport. He complained to God, "Why are you doing all these terrible things to me? I'm a nice fellow. I lead a good life. I don't deserve all this grief."

St. Brigid, who was also at the airport (she's often there, you know, disguised as a passenger agent), came over to him and said, "Hey, Mister, you have a nice home. You can afford a new car. Your garage and antenna are insured. You have a wonderful wife and great kids, even if they are sick sometimes. And your dog did come home. Now you have three days of peace here at the airport. You could thank God for all his blessings instead of complaining, right? You might even learn to laugh a little at how silly you sound."

And the man did.

(AG)

Calling Mr. Right

> "Therefore, keep awake—for you do not know when the master of the house will come, in the evening, or at midnight, or at cockcrow, or at dawn, or else he may find you asleep when he comes suddenly. And what I say to you I say to all: Keep awake."
>
> *Mark 13:35-37*

Once upon a time, there was a teenage girl named Belinda. She was somewhat interested in a boy named Randolph, a nice, smart, respectful boy, and a good dancer too. (You know how few teenage boys are good dancers.)

Randolph paid no attention to Belinda, but she didn't care because she wasn't really sure that she liked him. Then Randolph began to call her on the phone every night for a whole week.

"Why don't you call that nice boy Randolph back?" her mother asked.

"He's a creep," Belinda insisted. "He's boring!"

Of course, Belinda had every intention of calling Randolph back, but she didn't want to appear too eager. So finally, on Saturday afternoon, she called him back, but he wasn't in. She called him on Sunday afternoon, and he still wasn't in. Furious, she called him Sunday night and got him.

"I hear you have been calling me on the phone, Randolph," Belinda said in a snippy tone of voice.

"I'm sorry you didn't call me back earlier, Belinda," Randolph said sadly. "I was gonna invite you to the homecoming dance at school. But since you didn't return my calls, I figured you didn't want to go. So I asked someone else. Maybe some other time?"

"I'm a total space cadet," Belinda said to herself after she hung up.

You never know when Mr. Right is going to call with an invitation to dance.

(AG)

Do You Love Me?

"The words that I have spoken to you are spirit and life. But among you there are some who do not believe."

John 6:63-64

Once upon a time, a young couple named Mike and Jennifer were preparing for their marriage. They loved each other, they thought, and they were sure their marriage would be a happy one.

Unfortunately, Mike was the suspicious and jealous type. He wanted to keep track of Jennifer at all times. He demanded to know everything she was doing and expected her to give him a detailed account of every conversation she had and every person she met.

Jennifer soon became weary of these demands. "Will you keep asking those questions after we're married?" she asked.

"Of course I will," Mike replied.

"Why?" Jennifer wanted to know.

"Because I will want to be sure that you still love me," Mike explained.

"But how can I prove that if you don't already

26

believe it?" Jennifer said.

"It's part of a wife's job to let her husband know she loves him every day," Mike insisted.

"Do you have to do the same thing for me?" Jennifer asked.

"Of course not," Mike laughed.

"Why not?" said Jennifer.

"Because you're already sure that I love you," said Mike.

Jennifer gave Mike back the ring.

(AG)

Fathers and Sons

Jesus said to them again, "Peace be with you.
As the Father has sent me, so I send you."

John 20:21

A Chicago taxi driver, a native of Turkey, told this story, swearing it could be found in the Koran. Once a son, who had assumed the obligation of caring for his elderly father, began to worry about this responsibility. The son, knowing he had barely enough resources to care for himself, his wife, and his family, soon felt the added burden of the father's loss of sight. Having to lead the old man around took time away from what the son felt were more pressing responsibilities.

The son fretted over what he could do. Finally, exasperated by the demands his father placed both on his time and his resources, the son resorted to a drastic solution. He offered to take his father for a walk to the nearby sea. The son led his father up the hill by the seaside. As they approached the edge of the hill, he failed to warn his father of the drop ahead of them. The father died from the fall into the swirling sea waves.

The story goes on to tell how the son's action is repeated through many generations of his family, each son eventually experiencing the fate of his own father. Finally one day as a son and father begin the journey to the sea, the father turned to the son and said, "Son, I know where we are going, and I know what you plan for me. It is not necessary for you to take me there. I can find my way to the sea and will do what you want me to do. Go home to your family and do not worry."

The son, ashamed of his proposed deed, asked the father why he would offer to do such a thing. The father responded, "I did the same thing to my father that he had done to his father, and it has been done so for many generations. But if I go on my own, perhaps your son will not know of this solution when you are a burden to him."

The son wept at his father's words and begged his forgiveness. He then brought the father back to his home, where the old man taught his son new ways to increase the family's meager income. His daughter-in-law and grandchildren gained many new insights into the wisdom of the old man, and when his son reached his old age, he and his wife were welcomed into their son's home.

(MD)

Friends

"You are my friends if you do what I command you. I do not call you servants any longer, because the servant does not know what the master is doing; but I have called you friends, because I have made known to you every-thing that I have heard from my Father."

John 15:14-15

Most high-school reunions are pretty horrible. Yet once upon a time, there was a fiftieth reunion of a high-school class. Everyone was in their middle or late sixties, yet they had no trouble remembering one another. The reunion was a grace for all because everyone felt young again, at least for a day.

Two men, who had been inseparable through grammar school and high school but had had a fight on graduation day, met each other for the first time in fifty years. They grinned, shook hands, and then, with the new emotional freedom that some men (even those in their sixties) have learned from their wives, they hugged each other.

The two spent the rest of the day laughing together about the good times they had enjoyed when they were young—so much fun, so many good times, so much happiness. They talked about all the years since then: the excitement and terror of the war, the surprise of prosperity after the war, happiness despite strain in their marriages, problems and triumphs with their children and grandchildren.

It seemed that somehow they had eliminated the separation of a half century. It was almost as if they had been close friends all those fifty years.

"What was the fight about?" the wife of one of them asked her husband as they were on their way home.

"Neither of us could remember," her husband replied. Turns out we couldn't get away from our friendship no matter how hard we tried."

Such is the nature of the friendship Jesus promised us.

(AG)

Getting Even

"You have heard that it was said, 'An eye for an eye and a tooth for a tooth.' But I say to you, Do not resist an evildoer. But if anyone strikes you on the right cheek, turn the other also; and if anyone wants to sue you and take your coat, give your cloak as well; and if anyone forces you to go one mile, go also the second mile."

Matthew 5:38-41

Once upon a time, a young boy grew up bitterly angry at the girl down the street. He was bright enough but slow-spoken and shy. She was quick-witted and witty. He said and did stupid things, was tongue-tied in class, stumbled on the playground, and was terrible in sports.

The girl laughed at him and made fun of him. He resented her popularity and intelligence and success. It was not right that she was so good at everything and he was so bad.

Then the other boys began to notice how pretty she was, and they all chased after her. Some of the girls began to like the shy boy, but the girl down the street labeled him a nerd and so they all agreed.

Finally, the boy's family moved away. He was glad to leave the neighborhood. He hated everyone in it, and he hated her especially. In his new neighborhood he was treated like everyone else. He stopped stumbling, he thought more quickly, he got good marks in class, he became popular.

The boy decided that it was all the girl's fault that he had not been popular in the old neighborhood. She had ruined the early part of his life. Someday he'd get even.

Many years later, the boy—now a young man—went to college, he met the girl—now a young woman—again. She was still beautiful and acted very friendly to him. She didn't seem to remember how cruel she had been. In fact, she even indicated she'd like to go out with him.

But the young man turned his back on the young woman and ignored her.

Thus did he get even.

Or did he?

(AG)

"Got It!"

> Then one of them, when he saw that he was healed, turned back, praising God with a loud voice. He prostrated himself at Jesus' feet and thanked him. And he was a Samaritan.
>
> *Luke 17:15-16*

Once upon a time, there was a man in his early thirties who was diagnosed with brain cancer. He had a wife and young children and a promising career.

Suddenly all of that was swept away from him. The man could barely talk or walk. He was in constant agony. His friends avoided him because they didn't know what to say.

The doctors shook their heads. It was too bad, but there was nothing they could do. At last a very famous doctor offered to operate on the man, even though everyone else had said the tumor was inoperable. The doctor warned the patient and his wife that he could very well die during the operation, though the doctor was pretty sure the man would survive and return to health.

The couple decided that they should take the

risk. After nine hours of surgery, the doctor came into the waiting room, grinned at the man's wife, and said, "Got it!"

The man recovered completely and went on to a happy and successful life. Twenty years later the surgeon died.

"We should go to the wake," the man's wife said.

"I'd like to," her husband replied, "but it's on Saturday, and I have an important golf tournament."

Apparently, the man didn't "get it."

(AG)

Grandmother Spider

> "Holy Father, protect them in your name that you have given me, so that they may be one, as we are one. While I was with them, I protected them in your name that you have given me. I guarded them, and not one of them was lost."
>
> *John 17:11-12*

A Native American tale about Grandmother Spider reminds us of Pope John Paul I's words: "God is Father, but, especially, Mother."

A long time ago when all the Spirits lived in the sky and all the creatures lived below on the earth, the creatures were secure because they felt protected by the sky above them. However, one day they noticed that the sky was moving away from them, and they became very frightened. How could they continue to exist if the Spirits were to abandon them?

So after many days of worrying, the creatures gathered around the campfire and wondered what they might do. Bear came forward and said, "I am the strongest of all creatures. I will grab the sky and hold it in place and then we will be safe." But even with Bear holding on with all his strength, the sky was still able to continue its slow movement away from earth.

Next Coyote stepped forward. "I am the best trickster," he said. "I can trick anything. I will trick the sky into staying with us." But all of Coyote's tricks did not succeed in keeping sky where it belonged above the earth.

Finally, those around the campfire heard a meek little voice say, "I will try to keep sky joined to us." Everyone laughed when they saw Grandmother Spider crawl out of the tall grass. How could a lowly spider (and especially a woman spider) hope to do what had been impossible for mighty Bear and Coyote?

But Grandmother Spider paid no attention to their jeers. She just began spinning away until she had a very long string, which she aimed at the sky. On her third try, when she was almost completely exhausted, her string reached the sky and she climbed up to the sky, rested for a short time and then began spinning again. All day she spun her web, going down and then back up between sky and earth. Finally, at the end of the day, sky and earth were firmly connected once again.

(MD)

Greg's Gross Gift

> When he looked up and saw a large crowd coming toward him, Jesus said to Philip, "Where are we to buy bread for these people to eat?" He said this to test him, for he himself knew what he was going to do.
>
> *John 6:5-6*

Once upon a time, not so long ago, a teenage boy named Greg decided he would make ice cream for his friends. You might say that's silly. What teenage boy would make ice cream and why would he make it for anyone else, anyway?

Who knows why Greg decided to do it? But in any case, he went out and bought one of those ice-cream makers and studied recipe books for ice cream and decided he would make his ice cream out of twenty-two percent butterfat, which is "like, you know, totally gross."

The first time Greg made his ice cream, his friends thought it wasn't so bad. "Not as good as Baskin-Robbins, of course," they said, "but all right. Except why did you do vanilla? That's no fun at all."

So, since Greg was a chocolate freak anyway, he got the thickest, richest, darkest dark chocolate he could find, and he made the grossest, stickiest, gooiest chocolate ice cream that has ever existed on earth.

Some of the kids thought it looked really yucky, but Greg served it with raspberry sauce and whipped cream and they ate every last bit of it. Then they sang Greg's praises. Some of them said he should open a store.

"What will you make us tomorrow, Greg?" they asked.

The next day when the friends showed up, however, they found that Greg had made a light, delicate strawberry confection. They refused to eat it.

"Where is the gross chocolate?" they demanded.

"I can't be expected to do the same thing every day," Greg replied.

His friends stormed away angry. So Greg took up making pies for himself and his family.

(AG)

Holy Communion

When he was at the table with them, he took bread, blessed and broke it, and gave it to them. Then their eyes were opened, and they recognized him; and he vanished from their sight.

Luke 24:30-31

Once upon a time, a husband and a wife were having a lot of conflict with each other. They fought over money, they fought over the time they spent with their family, they fought over where they would go on their vacations, they fought over their children, and, of course, they fought over what the fights were about.

Of course, at one time the man and woman had been deeply in love. In fact, they thought that they were still in love. It's just that the conflicts had filled up the time that used to be devoted to love.

One night, however, the man suggested that they get a baby sitter and go out for dinner. The woman said they didn't have time for that anymore, but the man insisted. The meal turned out to be wonderful, and the couple relaxed and had a good time and great conversation and began to realize how silly their quarrels had become and how easy it would be to avoid them.

"You know," the wife said on the way home, "it was almost as though God were with us while we were eating, guiding us to see how foolish we've been."

"Maybe God was," her husband replied.

Maybe it's not just in church that Jesus is present among us.

(AG)

Just an Ordinary Man

> Jesus took with him Peter and James and
> John, and led them up a high mountain apart,
> by themselves. And he was transfigured be-
> fore them, and his clothes became dazzling
> white, such as no one on earth could bleach
> them. And there appeared to them Elijah with
> Moses, who were talking with Jesus. Then
> Peter said to Jesus, "Rabbi, it is good for us
> to be here; let us make three dwellings, one
> for you, one for Moses, and one for Elijah."
>
> *Mark 9:2-5*

To say that Tom was from a dysfunctional family
would be an understatement. His father had died
early, a victim of alcohol addiction, an addiction
Tom's younger brother shared. His older sister was
on her third husband. His younger sister was living
with a man who refused to work and periodically
beat her. His mother was constantly calling him
either to help out one or the other of the siblings or
to complain about how hard her life was and that no
one ever helped her.

That Tom had managed to stay married for
more than twenty-five years, was a faithful husband, a good father to his four children, and also a

very successful businessman was amazing. In addition, he was always willing to lend a hand with both financial and emotional support when his mother or siblings were in need.

Needless to say, gratitude for this help was never expressed. His family always took it for granted that Tom should help them. (After all he was the "lucky" one.)

So when Tom was named his community's "Man of the Year" and honored at a black-tie dinner, his mother and brother and sisters refused to attend. They claimed he was "putting on airs" by inviting them to such a function. Among themselves they agreed that he must have bought the honor. Why else, they said, would anyone find someone so ordinary as Tom to be special?

(MD)

Love at Second Sight

> (The crowd said to him,) "Our ancestors ate the manna in the wilderness; as it is written, 'He gave them bread from heaven to eat.'" Then Jesus said to them, "Very truly, I tell you, it was not Moses who gave you the bread from heaven, but it is my Father who gives you the true bread from heaven. For the bread of God is that which comes down from heaven and gives life to the world."
>
> *John 6:31-33*

Once upon a time, there were two young people who fell in love at a resort in the middle of summer. They were convinced that this affection was the love of their lives. They promised that they would love each other forever. They would write after they went back to college, they would attend each other's homecoming dances in the fall, they would see each other at Thanksgiving and Christmas. Their hunger for each other would always exist.

Alas, as the cynical Brazilian proverb puts it, "Love is forever, but it does not last."

By Christmas, the couple's eternal love was forgotten. Eventually they each married other lovers and forgot about each other . . . almost. There was always a little part of their memories in which the other remained. It was foolish summer love, they realized, but it had been too sweet to forget completely.

Many, many years later, when both their families were raised and they were widow and widower, they met and fell in love again. Or perhaps they merely rediscovered that corner of their memories where their love had always persisted.

And so, although they were now much older, the two of them married and lived happily ever after.

Some love, you see, does last. The hunger for it just takes a while to be filled.

(AG)

Measure for Measure

> "Do not judge, and you will not be judged; do not condemn, and you will not be condemned. Forgive, and you will be forgiven; give, and it will be given to you. A good measure, pressed down, shaken together, running over, will be put into your lap; for the measure you give will be the measure you get back."
>
> *Luke 6:37-38*

Once upon a time, not so very long ago, there was a mother who was a master at manipulating her children—with serious negative consequences for all of them as they grew to adulthood.

Even after her children were grown, this mom continued to stir up dissent among them. In addition, she tried to alienate them from their father, whom she had divorced. After a time and with the help of counseling, the children came to realize the games their mother played and severely limited their contact with her. Still, she continued to cause havoc in their lives, spreading negative stories about them to their own children.

In short, she was a very difficult person; and as she aged her negative behavior became even more intense. Two of her three children began to see her only once or twice a year. Their lives were complicated enough with problems that they attributed to her, and their anger at her made it impossible for them to take responsibility for their own lives.

Eventually, as the woman entered her nineties and became somewhat disabled, the task of caring for her fell on the one daughter who had, with the support of her husband, been able to come to some understanding of why her mother was the way she was. Still, until the day the mother died, she continued to deride this daughter for not doing enough for her.

When the mother died, however, the two absent children experienced great guilt that made their lives even more complicated. But even though caring for her mother had been an onerous task, the caretaker daughter experienced a sense of peace she had not anticipated.

Perhaps the measure she had measured had finally been measured back to her.

(MD)

Murderer

"You have heard that it was said, 'You shall love your neighbor and hate your enemy.' But I say to you, Love your enemies and pray for those who persecute you, so that you may be children of your Father in heaven."

Matthew 5:43-45

Once upon a time, a teenage boy was driving down the street in his father's car and not really watching where he was going. A little girl, three years old, ran into the street, and the car hit and killed her.

The police said that it wasn't the boy's fault, because there was no way he could have seen the girl until the last second. Still, the boy was not sure that he was not to blame. He tried to apologize to the girl's parents when they came out of church after her funeral, but they wouldn't accept his apology. They screamed at him and said that they hoped he suffered for the rest of his life just as they would and that he should burn in hell for all eternity for what he did.

The parents sued the boy, and the case was settled out of court by the insurance companies.

But the parents continued to curse the boy whenever they saw him. One of their friends said to them, "You're both good Christians, aren't you supposed to forgive?"

"Never!" they both shouted. "Being a Christian doesn't mean you have to forgive a murderer."

"Isn't that exactly what Jesus did?" asked the friend.

(AG)

Nice Guys Finish First

> (Gabriel said,) "For nothing is impossible with God." Then Mary said, "Here am I, the servant of the Lord; let it be with me according to your word."
>
> *Luke 1:37-38*

Once upon a time, there was a company that was in a bad way. The last three CEOs had been dummies. The company's stock had lost sixty percent of its value, its market share had declined by thirty percent, its bright people were leaving, and morale among the employees was at rock bottom.

The product the company made was still the best in the market. But the previous top executives had been lazy and mean and had spent most of their time awarding themselves and their friends huge bonuses. They paid no attention to advertising or marketing. Finally a new board of directors was appointed at the stockholders' insistence. They fired the CEO with a thunderous denunciation. They warned the employees that all their jobs—and their pensions—were in grave jeopardy. The workers were terrified.

Finally, the new CEO arrived. He was expected to fire half the workers, cut back on expenses, and give the company the good shaking that everyone said it needed. Instead he walked around the building, smiled at everyone, assured everyone that everything would be all right and that he didn't plan to fire anyone. "Another fool," they said around the water coolers.

Then the CEO met with the managers and the union leaders to get their suggestions and commitment. They confirmed that their product was the best in the business and that their workforce was ready to work.

So the CEO hired a new marketing director, brought in a new advertising and public-relations firm, and launched a very clever television campaign. Everyone in the company began to admire their boss and work hard for him. In six months the company was well on the way to recovery.

"Some nice guys finish first," they now say around the water cooler. The new CEO merely says, "The fear of the Lord is the beginning of wisdom . . . but only the beginning."

(AG)

Only Good Things

"Is there anyone among you who, if your child asks for a fish, will give a snake instead of a fish? Or if the child asks for an egg, will give a scorpion? If you then, who are evil, know how to give good gifts to your children, how much more will the heavenly Father give the Holy Spirit to those who ask him!"

Luke 11:11-13

Once upon a time, not too many years ago, John, a young man in his early forties, lay dying, consumed by the last stages of cancer that had spread to his liver. His wife and two young teenage sons, along with his parents, who had come from Ireland, and his siblings from all over the United States were at his bedside, reciting the rosary over and over.

For more than three years, these people and many other friends and relatives of John had stormed the heavens, praying that he would beat the cancer. As John became more and more ill, however, it seemed that those prayers had been in vain. Still, his loved ones never gave up.

When at last John slipped away quite peacefully, his mother observed in her Irish brogue, "Sure now, didn't we pray Johnny into heaven, and wasn't it a good thing for us to be here and see him going home? Now the Good Lord's going to have to help us make it through life without John. And Johnny himself will have to intervene for us."

(MD)

Paschal's New Wager?

> While (Jesus) was praying, the appearance
> of his face changed, and his clothes became
> dazzling white.
>
> *Luke 9:29*

Once there was a scientist who believed in nothing at all. He enjoyed especially putting down those who had near-death experiences in which they were revived after they had clinically died.

It was all brain chemistry, the scientist insisted, an evolutionary adjustment by a species that was conscious of its own mortality. There was no long dark tunnel, no figure in white at the end of it, no choice about whether to stay or come back. It was all an illusion caused by the brain chemicals that were released at the moment of death.

Then the man had a heart attack. He was clinically dead by the time they got him to the hospital. The doctors were able to revive him, however, and the scientist—ever faithful to his profession—dutifully reported that he had indeed gone through a near-death experience himself.

"It was only an illusion," he insisted. "I still do

not believe in life after death. When we are dead, we are dead, and that's that."

For some reason, however, after that experience the man seemed noticeably less afraid of death than most of his atheist colleagues. One of them asked him if he was not afraid that he might be wrong, that maybe there really is something after death.

"Promise you won't quote me?" the scientist asked. "Well, I figure that if my near-death experience was all an illusion, then I have nothing to lose by saying it was an illusion. On the other hand, if the person in white that the brain chemicals made me imagine is real, then there's so much love there that I have nothing to lose by denying it, because I will be forgiven."

"Oh," said his colleague.

(AG)

St. "Bride"

> "Whoever welcomes a prophet in the name
> of a prophet will receive a prophet's reward;
> and whoever welcomes a righteous person
> will receive the reward of the righteous; and
> whoever gives even a cup of cold water to
> one of these little ones in the name of a dis-
> ciple—truly I tell you, none of these will lose
> their reward."
>
> *Matthew 10:41-42*

This is one of the many stories of St. Brigid or "Bride" as she is known in Ireland. Brigid was the daughter of a noble pagan who sold her mother, his Christian concubine, to a druid when he learned of her pregnancy. It is said that once Brigid was of an age to fix her mind on God, all she asked for was granted. And this was no small thing because what she asked for was to satisfy the poor, house the homeless, bring diverse groups together, expel hardship, and spare the miserable.

As a young girl, her chore was to churn the butter for the druid's household. When the druid and his wife came to claim their butter, they discovered that Brigid was giving the butter to the poor and sick. They also discovered that the butter kept multiplying, so there was always enough for them, too. This moved the druid to give Brigid and her mother their freedom. He also convinced her noble father to accept the girl.

Once back in her father's house, however, Brigid began giving his things to the poor. She also resolutely refused to marry, a right that the law of her time and place gave her. Fearful that his daughter would give away all he had, the father decided to circumvent the law by selling her back into slavery to the king of Leinster, who had recently converted to Christianity.

While her father negotiated with the king, Brigid was outside giving her father's best sword to the first beggar who came along! She incensed both her father and the king by saying that she did this because the sword was used for war and the beggar would sell it for food. The king declared he wanted no part of Brigid's giving away all his wealth. Suddenly, a great flame appeared behind Brigid as she told him that if she had his wealth, she would give it to the Lord of the Elements and to the people who are the Lord's. The heat of the flame caused the king to break into a sweat that reminded him of the waters of his baptism. The king then insisted that her father leave her be, giving Brigid the freedom to commit herself to a life dedicated to God.

(MD)

Scarlet Ribbons

> Martha said to Jesus, "Lord, if you had been here, my brother would not have died. But even now I know that God will give you whatever you ask of him." Jesus said to her, "Your brother will rise again."
>
> *John 11:21-23*

A young mother, exhausted after overseeing nine seven-year-old boys at her son's birthday party, decided to take a well-deserved nap. The birthday was in the winter, a few days after the end of the holiday season, the second one since her father's death.

When the woman awoke from the nap, she remained in bed, deciding to savor a few more moments of peace and quiet. Suddenly out of nowhere, she heard—quite clearly she says—the music to "Scarlet Ribbons," a song her father used to sing when the family went for a long drive. At the same time, she felt what she describes as "an incredible sense of happiness, the feeling that Dad was telling me that the peace I felt just lying there was how he felt when he died."

The woman had explained to her family at

the time of her father's death that it seemed to her his last breath was one of great agony. Though other family members had described the scene as similar to the moment of birth, she had always had a hard time discarding her negative image of that moment.

But now she is convinced that the Scarlet Ribbons experience was her father's way of calming her fear and telling her that when he died he had also come to life in a new way.

Like Jesus did to Martha, he came to tell her that we never really die.

(MD)

Special Knowledge

When (Jesus) came to Nazareth, where he
had been brought up, he went to the syna-
gogue on the sabbath day, as was his cus-
tom. He stood up to read, and the scroll of the
prophet Isaiah was given to him. He unrolled
the scroll and found the place where it was
written:
The Spirit of the Lord is upon me,
because he has anointed me
to bring good news to the poor.
He has sent me to proclaim
release to the captives
and recovery of sight to the blind,
to let the oppressed go free,
to proclaim the year of the Lord's favor."

Luke 4:16-19

Once upon a time, a father and his five-year-old
daughter saw a rainbow. The father, a man with a
scientific mind, explained to the girl how rainbows
formed.

When they returned home, the girl, who not
only believed everything her father said but who
also was very bright, explained to her mother and
other siblings how rainbows formed.

One day in the girl's kindergarten class, a ray
of sun hit the metal on the fish tank and one of the

know-it-all boys in the room announced that it was a rainbow. The little girl was quick to point out that it was definitely not a rainbow. She then gave her father's explanation of how rainbows actually form.

The boy, who did not like being corrected—especially by a girl—responded that she was wrong. The girl insisted she was right. Her daddy had told her.

The boy's response was, "Your daddy is stupid!"

Even kindergartners do not like one of their own having special knowledge.

(MD)

Strangers and Friends

When the angels had left them and gone into heaven, the shepherds said to one another, "Let us go now to Bethlehem and see this thing that has taken place, which the Lord has made known to us."

Luke 2:15

Once upon a time, not so very long ago, a young mother gave birth to a tiny baby girl who had a heart defect. The doctor at the hospital said the baby would need special medical attention if she were to live.

The mother, a recent immigrant whose husband was unemployed, worried about how they might get help for their beautiful little baby. In addition to being financially strapped, they had an active two-year-old at home and no relatives in the country to help them.

A young girl, a "candy striper" volunteer, overhearing the conversation between the doctor and the new mother, told the story at her family dinner table. Later that evening the girl's mother went to the hospital to see what help the family needed.

The next day the mother organized a group of her friends to help care for the couple's two-year-old and the candy striper and her friends were recruited to baby-sit when their mothers were not available. The women also arranged for their church guild to give the family financial support.

The new parents, the helping women, and the candy striper and her friends all had a grand celebration when a healthy Baby Maria was finally released from the hospital. The baby's parents tell everyone they meet about the kindness of people who were strangers but are now friends.

(MD)

The Advance Man

> There was a man sent from God, whose name was John. He came as a witness to testify to the light, so that all might believe through him. He himself was not the light, but he came to testify to the light.
>
> *John 1:6-8*

Once upon a time, there was a politician who was running in a very close election. He had a good message and an exciting platform, but he was not well known. Thus he had to make a lot of speeches around the district, go to many meetings, attend tea parties and receptions and cocktail parties and church gatherings.

A good friend of the candidate was his advance man—the fellow who made all the arrangements and planned all the logistics for the campaign.

Unfortunately, he was not a very good advance man; rather he was unreliable and pompous and, worst of all, disorganized. The other people in the campaign hated him, but the candidate stuck with his friend. As the election drew near, the polls showed the candidate losing ground. The advance man knew they were going to lose, so he gave up altogether. The campaign self-destructed in the last week.

Yet the candidate lost by only one half of one percent of the votes. All the media people said that if the campaign had been better organized, the voters would have gotten to know the candidate better and he would have won in a walk.

We're supposed to be advance persons for Jesus. Sometimes you have to wonder why he doesn't fire us.

(AG)

The Best Christmas Ever

When they had finished everything required
by the law of the Lord, they returned to Gali-
lee, to their own town of Nazareth. The child
grew and became strong, filled with wisdom;
and the favor of God was upon him.

Luke 2:39-40

Christmas the year Nora was eight was a day
she will always remember. You see, Nora loved
Christmas. Surprisingly, the gifts she received were
not the main reason, although she was not op-
posed to receiving gifts and always left out cookies
and hot chocolate for Santa. What she loved most
about Christmas were the decorations and the
music and the crèche at church and the big family
gathering at Grandma and Grandpa's house. The
birthday celebration for the Christ Child was her
idea of a perfect birthday party, one she looked
forward to with eager anticipation.

A week or so before Christmas that year,
however, Nora overheard her mother say to her
grandmother, "I'm afraid Christmas just won't be the
same for Nora this year. I think she knows and is
just pretending." Nora wasn't quite sure what her

mother meant. She remembered her mother saying that Grandpa might not feel up to having big crowds around after his recent operation. Maybe Grandma told her mother that they would not be having the family Christmas party and her mother hadn't told her.

Nora didn't want to cause her mother to worry more about Grandpa, so she didn't ask about the Christmas plans. Still, she was very sad that they would not be having a big family birthday celebration for Jesus. She kept hoping Grandpa would feel better or one of the aunts would have the party or maybe even her mother would have it.

Imagine Nora's surprise and delight on Christmas Day when, after opening their gifts from Santa and going to church, they began packing the car with gifts and food and headed for Grandma and Grandpa's house. She no longer felt sad. Her prayers had been answered. When Nora went to bed that night, she wondered why her mother thought this would not be a good Christmas for her. It was her best Christmas ever.

Whenever Nora remembers that Christmas, she smiles, knowing now what her mother was worrying about. Adults can be so silly sometimes!

(MD)

The Boy and His Dog

> From that time on, Jesus began to show his disciples that he must go to Jerusalem and undergo great suffering at the hands of the elders and chief priests and scribes, and be killed, and on the third day be raised. And Peter took him aside and began to rebuke him, saying, "God forbid it, Lord! This must never happen to you." But he turned and said to Peter, "Get behind me, Satan! You are a stumbling block to me; for you are setting your mind not on divine things but on human things."
>
> *Matthew 16:21-23*

Once upon a time, there was a little boy whose dog was killed by a car. The boy was furious at the man who drove the car. He shouted at him and hit him.

"I didn't mean to do it," said the man.

"But you did do it," said the boy, "and I hate you."

This was the first time the boy had ever seen anything that was dead, and his dog was very dear to him. The boy's mother tried to explain to him that everything living must die someday.

"If you live, then you will die," she said, as

gently as she could. "Some day Daddy and I will die, just like your grandma and grandpa you never knew. Some day you will die too. But we believe that love is as strong as death, so nothing that God loves ever really dies."

The little boy thought about it for a while and then asked his mom whether God loved his dog. The mommy said that she was sure God did.

"So then doggy really isn't dead," he exclaimed.

His mother reached for an answer. "Everything that is in the mind of God exists forever," she said.

The little boy brightened. "Then everything will be all right," he said.

"Yes," said the mommy. "Everything will be all right, and all manner of things will be all right."

(AG)

The Confused Marble Player

> Jesus, looking at (the man), loved him and said, "You lack one thing; go, sell what you own, and give the money to the poor, and you will have treasure in heaven; then come, follow me." When he heard this, he was shocked and went away grieving, for he had many possessions.
>
> *Mark 10:21-22*

Once upon a time, there was a little boy who loved to play marbles.

This young man, whose name was Adelbert, was a very good marble player. In fact, he was devastating. He won every marble match during the first month of school and cleaned out all his friends. Pretty soon he was the only kid who had any marbles left.

Then the other boys bought more marbles and came back to take on Adelbert again. He cleaned them out a second time.

Every day, Adelbert would take all his marbles from the great big bags he stored them in and pour them out on the floor of his family's recreation room just to look at them.

His mother said, "Adie, why are you so obsessed with the marbles?"

"Because they are so beautiful," Adelbert said, his eyes glowing.

The other kids came back with more marbles for a third round, but suddenly Adelbert refused to play anymore. He was too busy admiring the marbles he had won.

"I have all the marbles I need," he told the others. "It's more fun to just look at my big bags of marbles than to waste my time playing with you drips."

Thus did Adelbert confuse the ends with the means.

(AG)

The Contentious Party

> Martha was distracted by her many tasks; so she came to (Jesus) and asked, "Lord, do you not care that my sister has left me to do all the work by myself? Tell her then to help me." But the Lord answered her, "Martha, Martha, you are worried and distracted by many things; there is need of only one thing."
>
> *Luke 10:40-42*

Once upon a time, a woman decided that on the last weekend of the summer she would have a party for the neighbors at the family's summer place in gratitude for what good friends they had been. She hoped that this would become an annual tradition.

"Let's have pizza," her kids said (as they always say).

"We can grill some hamburgers," her husband said. "That's easy" (which is what he always says).

"No," said the woman. "We should give a really nice dinner (which is what she always says).

The rest of the family groaned because they knew what that meant—a whole day of hard work for everyone, during which the woman would act like the party wasn't her idea but theirs and complain that they weren't helping enough.

The others thought that beef Welllington was a little much for a summer dinner. They saw no reason to clean up the house as if it were Christmastime. They argued that if they had to have caesar salad, couldn't it come out of a bag? Was it really necessary to bake potatoes? Wouldn't potato salad be just as good? Couldn't they buy the apple pies at the bakery instead of making a half dozen of them? And what was wrong with packaged pie crust? On and on the disagreements went.

Well, as usual, the woman's party was a feast that all the guests enjoyed.

The woman would have enjoyed it a lot more, however, if she wasn't so worn out from fighting with her family about it.

(AG)

The Cynic

> Jesus said, "I came into this world for judgment so that those who do not see may see, and those who do see may become blind." Some of the Pharisees near him heard this and said to him, "Surely we are not blind, are we?" Jesus said to them, "If you were blind, you would not have sin. But now that you say, 'We see,' your sin remains."
>
> *John 9:39-41*

Once upon a time, there lived a woman who was a cynic. Even as a little girl, she was suspicious of everyone. Everybody, she figured, had an angle, a hidden agenda, a trick up the sleeve.

Someone had told her when she was fourteen that she was a paranoid. She had replied (unbeknownst to her, she was quoting William Burroughs, whom she hadn't read), "A paranoid is someone who is just beginning to understand how things really work."

Whenever anyone did anything nice for the woman, she suspected that they were somehow trying to exploit her. She believed that gifts and compliments she received were based on some terrible secret motive.

Eventually the woman married a very nice man and had a very nice family, all of whom claimed to love her, praised her on every possible occasion, and showered her with gifts. She continued to think that even her family was all part of the conspiracy against her. As cynical as the woman was, however, they weren't turned off, because—except for her cynicism—she really was a very nice person.

Finally, on her deathbed, surrounded by children and grandchildren and great-grandchildren, the woman finally admitted, "Well, I guess you did love me after all."

(AG)

The Demanding Boss

"Come to me, all you that are weary and are carrying heavy burdens, and I will give you rest. Take my yoke upon you, and learn from me; for I am gentle and humble in heart, and you will find rest for your souls. For my yoke is easy, and my burden is light."

Matthew 11:28-30

Once upon a time, there was an administrative assistant. He was not the most ambitious or reliable person in the world, but he tried hard . . . at least some of the time.

The man's boss was generous and good-hearted, because it was in her nature to do so. When she corrected the man's mistakes, she did so very gently. When holidays fell in the middle of the week, she gave him the rest of the week off. She even let him take the week after Christmas off because, as she put it, "Nothing ever gets done that week anyhow."

On summer Fridays, the boss let the administrative assistant leave at noon. Whenever he needed time to go to the doctor or to attend a family event, she gave it to him without question. She granted the man a substantial raise every year and wrote generous reports on him for his personnel file.

One day, however, the man quit without notice. He took what he thought was a better job with another company. He told his replacement, "You won't like working for her, she's too demanding."

(AG)

The Father of Ice Cream

"This is the bread that came down from heaven, not like that which your ancestors ate, and they died. But the one who eats this bread will live forever."

John 6:58

Storyteller John Shea tells of a father who brought his four kids to an ice-cream parlor. Only three of them came inside. The teenage girl remained in the car sulking, because she was at that age of life at which teenage girls love to sulk.

Meanwhile, the two boys in the group fought over which one of them could choose first, because they both wanted garlic-chocolate-fudge-with-cookie-crumbles—and one could not (of course) order what the other had already ordered. (It was unthinkable!) So the two of them almost came to blows when the older boy did order that ice cream, and the younger one was constrained to settle for orange-ripple-pizza-flavored ice cream.

The little girl of the family (she couldn't have been more than four) wept because all the chocolate-chocolate-chocolate-chip was gone, and nothing would console her—not even a triple scoop of peppermint-fudge-raspberry-mango. She sobbed all through her destruction of the cone.

Finally, the teenager came in and sulked because they didn't have "anything," (though actually there were more than forty flavors). She finally settled on a single scoop of vanilla yogurt "in a dish" as a protest against the injustices of the human condition.

When they got home, however, the father told his wife how much fun he had had on their outing, and he was speaking the truth.

They were his children, you see, and he loved them.

And he delighted in feeding them.

(AG)

The Fight

> "I say to you that if you are angry with a brother or sister, you will be liable to judgment; and if you insult a brother or sister, you will be liable to the council; and if you say, 'You fool,' you will be liable to the hell of fire."
>
> *Matthew 5:22*

O nce upon a time, a husband and a wife had a big, big fight. None of their family or friends was quite sure what the fight was about since each time one or the other told the story it changed.

After a while, the couple began fighting about what the fight had been about and what the other person had said about the fight. Technically they were not talking to each other, but they talked enough to keep the fight going.

"Maybe I should get a divorce, if you're so fed up with me," the man said.

"Fine," said his wife, "only you take the kids!"

The couple's guardian angels had a summit conference and decided that something had to be done. They arranged for the husband's car to be bumped by a hit-and-run driver. The car was not badly damaged, but the husband had to spend two days in the hospital under observation.

Suddenly, the quarrel was quickly forgotten. "Sometimes I think I'd be better off without you," the wife said, "but this has made me face the real prospect of being without you, and I realize I would not be better off."

"Me, too," agreed the husband.

So the couple fell in love all over again.

(AG)

The Genius

> "Everyone therefore who acknowledges me before others, I also will acknowledge before my Father in heaven; but whoever denies me before others, I also will deny before my Father in heaven."
>
> *Matthew 10:32-33*

Once upon a time, there was a young woman who won every short-story contest she entered when she was in high school. She decided that she would be a great novelist some day and wanted to major in writing in college.

Her parents and siblings ridiculed her, however. "Who do you think you are?" they said. Then they added the clincher, "What will people say?"

So the woman majored in primary education, because her family said that everyone should have a useful career skill. But she hated college and flunked out. Then she went to a local community college and studied literature and creative writing. The family made fun of her again. "What good will that ever do?" they said. "How much money do writers make, anyway?"

They wanted her to go to graduate school in

business. She absolutely refused. They tried to get her a seat on the Board of Trade. She turned them down flat. Instead she got a job as a waitress and lived in a one-room apartment, where her only companion was her computer.

"You might as well be a nun," the family said. "We give up on you."

At twenty five, the woman published her first novel. It won the Pulitzer Prize and sold three million copies.

Her family took credit for her success. "We always had faith in her genius," they said.

(AG)

The Giver Who Changed Her Mind

> When the time came for their purification according to the law of Moses, they brought (Jesus) up to Jerusalem to present him to the Lord.
>
> *Luke 2:22*

Once upon a time, there was an eleven-year-old named Mary Elizabeth. She was a most excellent little girl. There were times, however, when Mary Elizabeth became angry. She erupted without notice, like a volcano. She would start loud and just get louder as she grew angrier and angrier.

Mary Elizabeth's had a friend named Angela. The two were inseparable. They promised each other that—no matter what—they would be best friends all their lives.

Before Angela's twelfth birthday, Mary Elizabeth spent two whole days shopping with her mother for just the right dress to give Angela. In fact, they returned two dresses they had purchased before Mary Elizabeth was satisfied it was the perfect one. And Angela loved the dress. She said it was the most beautiful thing she'd ever owned.

Two weeks later, however, Mary Elizabeth and Angela had a terrible fight—the kind only preteen girlfriends can have over who-knows-what forgettable issue. They cried and shouted at one another, screaming things like, "I'll hate you forever!"

The day after the fight, Mary Elizabeth stormed over to Angela's house and demanded the dress back. They fought and pulled each other's hair. Finally, Angela's mother shoved Mary Elizabeth out of the house, but Angela stood outside and yelled and yelled. Finally, Angela's mother called Mary Elizabeth's mother and told her to come over and get her daughter.

Mary Elizabeth's mother was very stern with her daughter. "You can't take gifts back just because you get angry at a friend," she said. "It's like giving something to God. Once you've done it, there's no turning back. It is God's forever."

(AG)

The Gourmet Dad

> While they were eating, he took a loaf of bread, and after blessing it he broke it, gave it to them, and said, "Take; this is my body." Then he took a cup, and after giving thanks he gave it to them, and all of them drank from it. He said to them, "This is my blood of the covenant, which is poured out for many."
>
> *Mark 14:22-24*

Once upon a time, not too long ago, there was a single dad who thought he was a renaissance man (some daddies are that way, you know). He played golf and basketball, he sang (especially at weddings, even when he wasn't invited), he wrote poetry, he painted, and he was skilled in the mysteries of the Internet. He thought there was nothing he could not do if he set his mind to it.

So one day the dad announced to his five children that he was going to become a gourmet cook. They all laughed at him, politely and lovingly, but they still laughed. So he was even more determined. He went to cooking class every week and practiced on the class and on some of his friends. Finally, one night he announced that on the following Sunday he would cook a feast for his family.

Now, all the kids had something else they would rather do that night, but because they loved their daddy, they came to the meal, suppressing (almost) their giggles.

To their astonishment, the meal was wonderful. So the kids went to their various schools on Monday and bragged that their daddy was the best cook in the world.

And he did it all, they said, because he loves us so much.

(AG)

The Great Feast

"When you give a banquet, invite the poor, the crippled, the lame, and the blind. And you will be blessed, because they cannot repay you, for you will be repaid at the resurrection of the righteous."

Luke 14:13-14

Once upon a time, a young couple began planning their wedding. They were soon overwhelmed by how expensive it would be to have even a simple party for all the people they hoped would come to celebrate this important occasion with them.

Both the bride and the groom had spent two years after college working as volunteers with very poor people. They found it hard to justify the expense of the wedding. Still, they felt that their wedding should be a time to gather their large families and many friends to witness their commitment and rejoice with them.

Finally, they decided on a way to celebrate with their family and friends and at the same time help people less fortunate than they were. They included a card in their wedding invitation, inviting their guests to help them help the poor and disabled by considering a donation to one of their favorite charities in lieu of a wedding gift.

The couple's concern for the poor touched many who received the invitation. Those who attended the wedding commented on how impressed they were by the thoughtfulness of the young couple. As a result of their idea, various charities received substantial donations—and the couple still got plenty of toasters and towels.

By all accounts, the wedding was a simple, but great, feast.

(MD)

The Great Leader

"Very truly, I tell you, the one who believes in me will also do the works that I do and, in fact, will do greater works than these, because I am going to the Father."

John 14:12

Once upon a time, a great leader decided that he had ruled his country long enough. He was still in the prime of life, but he had lost his wife, he felt his son was old enough to succeed him, and he wanted to spend the rest of his life in a monastery reading and writing, praying and reflecting.

Truth to tell, the leader was tired of the world, tired of the burdens of office, tired of the distractions of daily life. He called his family and advisers together and told them that it was time he stepped down. He said that he was growing rusty and stale on the job, that it was time for new leadership, new blood, new ideas, new vision.

Everyone protested, most of all the crown prince, who felt utterly inadequate to replace his father. The leader understood their reaction and was deeply moved by it. But, he insisted, it was time for him to withdraw, time to leave his family and friends on their own. He said that he had done his part in reorganizing the country and making it peaceful and prosperous. Now it was their turn to take over and champion all the things he had stood for during his life.

"I'll always be with you," he promised. "And if you ever need help—but I don't think you will—I will come back. But it is time for you to lead."

Jesus would have understood how the leader felt . . . and why he did what he did.

(AG)

The Grudge Counter

(Jesus) said to Thomas, "Put your finger here and see my hands. Reach out your hand and put it in my side. Do not doubt but believe."
John 20:27

Once upon a time, there was a man who counted carefully all his grudges. He remembered all the cruelties of the school yard, the taunts from his classmates when he did something well, the feather-brained irresponsibilities (as he saw them) of the young women he had dated, the dishonesty of his business associates, the insensitivity of his wife, the ingratitude of his children.

So many people had done such terrible things to this man that he figured there had to be a conspiracy. Who could have organized such a massive conspiracy against him?

Only God, the man concluded. For some reason, God did not like him. This was unfair, but what could the man do? If God had a grudge against him, that was that.

But then, he figured, he had the right to hold a grudge against God.

So the man held a grudge against God all his life. He died lonely and isolated, hated (he thought) by everyone who ought to have loved him.

"I have a grudge against you," he told God when he got to heaven.

"So what?" God replied. "I don't have a grudge against you."

Then God showed the man the scene at his funeral. All the people who the man thought had injured him were there. Many were crying, and they all were sad he had died, for in their own ways they had all loved him.

"Do you think maybe you missed the point?" God asked.

(AG)

The Killer Exam

> When (Peter) noticed the strong wind, he became frightened, and beginning to sink, he cried out, "Lord, save me!" Jesus immediately reached out his hand and caught him, saying to him, "You of little faith, why did you doubt?"
> *Matthew 14:30-31*

Once upon a time, there was a high-school physics teacher who gave very tough tests. But he was a good teacher and liked his students and wanted them to learn. So he emphasized the really important parts of the course and prepared his students for the exam.

He even told them that if they just listened carefully in class they would know everything they needed to know for the final exam. But the students didn't believe him. So they took copious notes of everything he said, and the words passed from his lectures to their notes without pausing in their memories.

When the time came for the test, most of the students went into an advanced stage of panic. They studied like crazy, poured over their notes, and even had study sessions in which groups of students would study together.

Three of the kids, however, didn't study at all because they hadn't taken any notes. They just paid attention and listened carefully in class, just like the teacher had told them. The night before the exam, they went to the movies.

The test was truly fearsome, but the three who hadn't study finished in a half hour and walked out of class confidently. The rest of the class went into a wild hysteria. They forgot everything about physics they ever knew. A few ended up with Ds; most of them flunked.

"Why didn't you listen to what I said?" the teacher asked. "O you of little faith!"

(AG)

The Lazy Quarterback

> "Whoever comes to me and does not hate father and mother, wife and children, brothers and sisters, yes, and even life itself, cannot be my disciple. Whoever does not carry the cross and follow me cannot be my disciple."
>
> *Luke 14:26-27*

Once upon a time, there was an eighth grader who was a great, great quarterback. Everyone said he'd make the high-school varsity team in his sophomore year—he was that good. They even said that when he graduated from high school he might go to Notre Dame!

Well, the kid was really good, but he was also lazy. Or maybe he just thought there were more important things to do with summer vacation than weight training and football practice. And maybe he was right.

He wanted to play football, you see, but he figured he was good enough that he could take the summer off and still make the team. So he didn't show up at the freshmen practices the first week in August or any week in August. When school started in September, he finally wandered down to the football field. He began to throw one perfect pass after another. The other freshmen on the team were enthused. There was even talk that maybe he would be picked for the varsity team as a freshman.

But the coach saw the boy and chased him off the field. "You didn't come to summer practice," the coach said, "so we don't want you now."

Maybe the coach was wrong, maybe there shouldn't be August football practice. But it is also true that if you don't want to work at something, no matter how good you are, you may be out of luck.

Maybe that's what Jesus meant when he said we had to give up everything to follow him.

(AG)

The Man Who Was Too Generous

> "Am I not allowed to do what I choose with what belongs to me? Or are you envious because I am generous?"
>
> *Matthew 20:15*

O nce upon a time, long, long ago, there was a village up in the mountains. In the early part of summer, a young man came up the mountain playing a happy little tune on a flute. The little kids followed after him. He played music for them and sang songs and told stories.

Pretty soon the teenagers joined the young man with the flute, and he taught them some new dances. One night, he announced that he was going to produce a play and invited the villagers to try out for him. The next night he had a song fest, and the night after that a storytelling contest, and the night after that a big dance for people of all ages.

The people in this village had never enjoyed long summer nights so much. Husbands and wives stopped quarreling; kids stopped lying to their parents; lovers were gentle with each other. All the villagers were astonished by the charm and the talent and the generosity of the young man.

After a couple of weeks, however, the few busybodies in the village who complained about everything began to complain about the young man. Who was he? Where did he come from? Who were his family? Why did he have so much free time in the summer? What was he up to? What kind of trick was he trying to play on them?

After a while, people in the village began to ignore the young man. Then some parents forbade their children to go near him. Teens began to insult him, and a few threw stones at him.

One night, a bunch of young toughs beat the flute player up and threw him out of town. Rumors spread that he was dead. But early the next morning, the village heard the flute again, this time playing a sad little tune as the young man who was too generous walked back down the mountain.

(AG)

The Man Who Would Be Head Usher

> Jesus called them and said to them, "You know that among the Gentiles those whom they recognize as their rulers lord it over them, and their great ones are tyrants over them. But it is not so among you; but whoever wishes to become great among you must be your servant; and whoever wishes to be first among you must be slave of all. For the Son of Man came not to be served but to serve, and to give his life as a ransom for many."
>
> *Mark 10:42-45*

Once upon a time, not too long ago, there was a man who worked for many years as an usher in a church. He came early every Sunday morning and sometimes worked as usher for three services. Everything was done efficiently when he was on duty.

Even though the man was not technically the head usher, he was the one who took the collection money from the other baskets and piled it into one basket to bring up to the altar. If some of the other ushers were slow or inefficient, the man didn't bother to hide his impatience. It was a privilege to be an usher, he felt, and one was supposed to work hard to live up to that privilege.

One day, the man who had been the head usher in the church since before the flood moved away. The other usher personally believed that the retiring man was a doddering old fool, but he had never said anything. Now, he assumed that his good work would be rewarded and that he would be made head usher. Then, finally, everything would be done efficiently, the way it was supposed to be.

But the pastor called a meeting of all the ushers and announced that a much younger man, a man who had worked as an usher for only two years, would be the new head usher.

Crestfallen, the man who would be head usher wrote a letter of resignation. And from then on, he went to a different church.

(AG)

The Miracle of the Flowers

Now the birth of Jesus the Messiah took place
in this way.

Matthew 1:18

Once Father Junipero Serra was riding through
the desert on his mule. It was a dark and cold
winter night. Though the desert usually was very
dry, it was snowing that night. He was worn out
from his travels and dead tired. All he wanted to do
was find a warm and peaceful place to sleep.

But in the darkness, the priest encountered a
young Native American man and his wife trying to
find their way through the snow on foot to a place of
shelter where the young woman could give birth to
her child. Father Junipero put her on his own mule
and led the two of them to a hut about which he
knew. He lit a fire for them and gave them some of
his food and water.

The priest immediately realized how similar
their situation was to that of Mary and Joseph. But
theirs was a miraculous situation, this was just a
poor couple in trouble. To give them privacy, Father
Junipero pitched his tent outside the house and

shivered underneath his blankets for most of the long night. He thought he heard a baby crying during the night, but he was so tired that he did not get up.

The next morning the sun was shining brightly, the air was warm, and the mule was grazing happily. Father Junipero remembered what had happened the night before. He rushed into the house, but the couple and their child were gone, and the room was filled with flowers. The priest took as many as he could carry back to his mission, where they bloomed for many months.

Whenever he told the story, Father Junipero said that he had no idea whether the couple were anything other than they appeared. What mattered was that they needed help and he could offer it.

(AG)

The Miser and
the Shoemaker

> "Then the king will say to those at his right
> hand, 'Come, you that are blessed by my Fa-
> ther, inherit the kingdom prepared for you from
> the foundation of the world; for I was hungry
> and you gave me food, I was thirsty and you
> gave me something to drink, I was a stranger
> and you welcomed me, I was naked and you
> gave me clothing, I was sick and you took care
> of me, I was in prison and you visited me.'"
> *Matthew 25:34-36*

A Jewish folk tale tells the story of a town miser
and a poor shoemaker.

The miser, a wealthy man, always refused to
help anyone in need. As a result, he was looked on
with disdain by all. Only beggars who were not from
the town would go to his door, unaware that this
man gave to no one. The poor shoemaker was
admired because he never turned a beggar away
from his door. When the miser died, no one even
bothered to pay their respects to such a selfish
man. Shortly after the miser's death, however, the
people of the town were amazed to hear that the
shoemaker was suddenly refusing to give assis-

tance to those in need. He claimed he no longer had money to give away.

This puzzled the townspeople, because they detected no difference in the shoemaker's situation. Worried about his apparent change of heart, they sought the advice of the rabbi. The rabbi went to question the shoemaker. Imagine the rabbi's surprise when the shoemaker told him that it was true that he had no money, that in fact he never gave away his own money . . . and he wasn't about to start now!

He told the rabbi that many years before, the man known as the miser had given him a large sum of money and asked him to give it to any beggar that came to him. His only request was that the shoemaker not reveal the source of the money while the miser was alive. Whenever the original donation ran out, the miser always replaced it. All those years it had been the miser's money, not his own, that the shoemaker had given away.

The shoemaker told the rabbi that he never understood how his fellow townspeople thought he had enough money to help people who came to him.

(MD)

The Mystery of the Manger

(Mary) gave birth to her firstborn son and wrapped him in bands of cloth, and laid him in a manger, because there was no place for them in the inn.

Luke 2:7

This is a story about how two eighth graders told a pastor what to say in his Christmas homily, and how that event became a parish legend.

Just before Midnight Mass at Nativity Church, Sister Pat and her eighth-grade class were in a terrible state. Jesus' statue from the church's crèche set was missing. For the first time in the 75 years that the parish had been celebrating both the birth of Jesus and its patron day, an eighth-grade girl, accompanied by an eighth-grade boy, was to carry the Baby Jesus in the entrance procession.

Mary Anne and Joey, who had been chosen to portray Mary and Joseph (not because of their names or because they were the smartest or best-looking kids in the class but because their names had been drawn from a hat), arrived early to once more (and for about the hundredth time as usual in parish schools) rehearse their roles.

When they went to take Jesus' statue from storage, it was gone. Sister Pat was very upset. What could they do now? Mary Anne and Joey approached her with their solution.

"You told us the manger is a feeding trough and reminds us that Jesus is the one who gives us the bread of life each time we come to the Eucharist," they said. "Why don't we put all the hosts into a basket and carry it in procession to the manger? Father Tom can talk about that in his homily and then we can bring the manger to the altar at the offertory procession."

Of course, the pastor did as he was told and everyone remarked, "What a marvelous homily!"

Then, after Communion, the statue mysteriously appeared in the manger, looking newer and brighter than anyone ever remembered. To this day, no one knows when or how it got there. So now the people of Nativity Parish have their very own Christmas legend, which they love to tell to all who will listen.

(MD)

The Optimistic Cub Fan

> (Jesus) left that place and came to his home-
> town, and his disciples followed him. On the
> sabbath he began to teach in the synagogue,
> and many who heard him were astounded.
> They said, "Where did this man get all this?
> What is the wisdom that has been given to
> him? What deeds of power are being done
> by his hands! Is not this the carpenter, the
> son of Mary and brother of James and Joses
> and Judas and Simon, and are not his sisters
> here with us?" And they took offense at him.
>
> *Mark 6:1-3*

This story is set in Chicago, but it could be set in
Boston, Cleveland, Seattle, San Diego, or any
number of long-suffering cities.

Not too long ago, a young man strolled in to
a Chicago sports bar with a tall stack of computer
print-outs. He laid the papers on the bar, pounded
the bar with a beer bottle, and announced, "Listen
up folks. I've got big news for you. I've developed a
new software program that predicts the major-
league baseball winners for the next three sum-
mers. It is absolutely certain that the Chicago Cubs
will win the pennant and the World Series three

years from now. I'll give ten-to-one odds. Do I have any takers?"

Everyone in the bar laughed and hooted. Who did this lunkhead think he was? He'd probably never been to a baseball game in his life. Didn't he know that it has been about a hundred years since the Cubs had last won a World Series? And all he had was his goofy computer program?

On and on they went. So the man had no trouble making lots and lots of bets.

Three years later, he made a ton of money.

(AG)

The Pastry Cook

> Taking the five loaves and the two fish, (Jesus) looked up to heaven, and blessed and broke the loaves, and gave them to the disciples, and the disciples gave them to the crowds.
>
> *Matthew 14:19*

Once a woman took a course in cooking pastries.

She learned how to make the most delightful sweet rolls and cakes and pies and tortes and fancy French goodies. They made your mouth water when you smelled them.

One Sunday, she made raisin danish for breakfast, linzer tortes for lunch, and a wonderful white chocolate mouse for supper.

But her husband and kids were boorish when it came to baking. All they wanted were chocolate-coated longjohns from Dunkin' Donuts.

So the mother, who loved her husband and children, bought chocolate-coated longjohns from Dunkin' Donuts the next Sunday.

She also made her wonderful pastries and brought them over to the church for the priests and nuns, who shared them with everyone.

(AG)

The Perfect Lovers

"My flesh is true food and my blood is true
drink. Those who eat my flesh and drink my
blood abide in me, and I in them."

John 6:55-56

Once upon a time, there was a young man who
was looking for the perfect young woman to be his
wife. One day he encountered a young woman who
was looking for the perfect young man. They both
turned on the charm and won each other over.
They fell hopelessly in love.

The couple told their families and friends that
they had each found the perfect spouse. The families and friends were skeptical. They knew that the
man and the woman were both nice young people,
but they were far from perfect!

Nor did the couple listen to the priest who
married them when he told them that God was the
only perfect lover.

"You don't understand," they told him in a
condescending tone of voice.

The couple got married, and by the time they
returned home from their honeymoon they were

sadly disillusioned. It turned out that neither of them was perfect, far from it. They knew then that the priest was right. Only God can satisfy the human heart completely. So they went to see the priest once again, to ask what they should do.

"If you try to become more gentle and patient and loving like God is, then you'll be more like God and therefore happier than you are now," he explained.

"That's hard to do," they replied.

"Who ever said love was easy?" asked the priest.

(AG)

The Poker Club

"Again, truly I tell you, if two of you agree on earth about anything you ask, it will be done for you by my Father in heaven. For where two or three are gathered in my name, I am there among them."

Matthew 18:19-20

Once upon a time, there was a club—four men who gathered together on the first Tuesday of each month to play penny-ante poker. Not much money ever changed hands, and all had a good time. One man brought the cards, another brought the chips, a third brought the beer, and a fourth brought popcorn. The wife of whoever was the host made sandwiches and then, with a sigh of relief, joined the other three wives at a movie.

One night, a wife tried to be little fancy and made hamburgers. The next time a different wife made pasta. The time after that, there was caesar salad, and the fourth time there were steaks. Now, you must not accuse the wives of starting the competition, because they were doing only what their husbands asked them to do.

Then the man whose turn it was to bring the

beer brought Guinness Stout instead of Budweiser or Miller, and the beer competition began. Then it was fancy potato chips and gourmet popcorn.

Pretty soon the poker club was split by rivalry and competition. Everyone tried to outdo everyone else. There was a fight at almost every session. The four men began first to dislike and then to hate one another. The poker club collapsed.

None of the men ever played poker again.

(AG)

The Quitter

Then the devil led (Jesus) up and showed him in an instant all the kingdoms of the world. And the devil said to him, "To you I will give their glory and all this authority; for it has been given over to me, and I give it to anyone I please. If you, then, will worship me, it will all be yours." Jesus answered him, "It is written,
'Worship the Lord your God,
and serve only him.'"

Luke 4:5-8

Once there was a famous movie actress who was talented, personable and beautiful. She won an Academy Award once and was nominated for one several times.

Moreover, both her talent and her beauty were durable. Everyone thought she would be able to play leading roles until she was at least sixty.

But on her fortieth birthday, the woman announced that she was retiring. She would make no more movies, give no more interviews, sign no more lucrative contracts. She wanted to be with her husband and her children, settle down in one place far from both Hollywood and New York, do volunteer work, and spend a lot of time reading and praying.

Everyone thought she was crazy. Wasn't she still a young woman? Shouldn't she make many more great films? Might not she be a good director or producer? Was it her family that made her retire?

"Nope," she said, "it was my idea, though my family likes it."

Was she afraid to grow old? Didn't she have half her life left?

"Yep," she said, "that's why I'm quitting now."

After she retired, people quickly forgot about her, almost as though she had died already.

That was just fine with her.

(AG)

The Reciprocal Invitation

> In the temple (Jesus) found people selling cattle, sheep, and doves, and the money changers seated at their tables. Making a whip of cords, he drove all of them out of the temple, both the sheep and the cattle. He also poured out the coins of the money changers and overturned their tables. He told those who were selling the doves, "Take these things out of here! Stop making my Father's house a marketplace!"
>
> *John 2:14-16*

Once upon a time, there was a little boy named Zack who refused to go to church with his family on Sunday.

"It's sooo boring!" Zack said to his parents. "I don't know what's happening. I don't like the music. I can't understand what they're reading out of those books. I don't know what the man in the funny clothes is talking about. And they won't let me play with my trucks. If God is there in church, I don't see him. Why can't I just talk to God in my own house while I'm watching *Sesame Street* or the Green Bay Packers?

Zack's parents tried to explain to him about

sacred space. God indeed is everywhere, they said, even when the TV is on. But he is especially in church. If we don't go to church on Sunday, then we might forget that God is in our home, and on *Sesame Street,* and even with the Green Bay Packers! If we don't go to church on Sunday, they told him, we're afraid we'll begin to forget about God during the rest of the week.

Zack didn't believe them, of course. So he decided to talk directly to God about it (with the TV off).

"I stop by your house all the time," God said to him. "Don't you think you might stop by mine once in a while?"

"Oh," Zack said. "Why didn't you put it that way before?"

So the boy started going to church every week without complaint.

And his parents never knew why.

(AG)

The Reluctant Singer

> When they found (Jesus), they said to him,
> "Everyone is searching for you." He answered,
> "Let us go on to the neighboring towns, so
> that I may proclaim the message there also;
> for that is what I came out to do."
>
> *Mark 1:37-38*

Once upon a time, there was a young man named Jimmy Mac. He was a commodity broker and a good one. Jimmy worked very hard, but commodity brokers don't work in the afternoon, so Jimmy spent his afternoon working on his voice.

That's right, Jimmy Mac had a fine tenor voice, and he wanted to improve it. He took lessons and practiced really hard and listened to recordings by lots of great singers. He didn't tell anyone about this interest, however, not his mother or his sisters or his friends or even the young woman he was kind of dating.

Jimmy Mac's voice was a deep, dark secret until one Saturday evening. At a wedding reception, when everyone had had a bit too much to drink, the bride and groom demanded that all the people in their wedding party sing a song. Jimmy was one of the ushers, and he was the last one to sing. He sang "I'll Take You Home Again, Kathleen," because the bride's name was Katie. He was fabulous.

Everyone was perfectly silent when Jimmy finished, and they broke out in a thunderous ovation. Even if they had had too much to drink, they knew great talent when they heard it.

The bride and groom wanted Jimmy to sing again, but he refused. Other people pleaded with him to sing at their weddings, but he refused. His mother, his father, his sisters, even his (kind of) girlfriend begged him to sing.

"No way," he said. "I sing only for myself, not for anyone else."

Jimmy's almost girlfriend said, "Go ahead and hide your light under a bushel."

(AG)

The Repentant Opponent

> John said to him, "Teacher, we saw someone casting out demons in your name, and we tried to stop him, because he was not following us." But Jesus said, "Do not stop him; for no one who does a deed of power in my name will be able soon afterward to speak evil of me. Whoever is not against us is for us."
>
> *Mark 9:38-40*

Once upon a time, a man and a woman were locked in a close primary race for their party's nomination to a political office. The woman was in the lead until a week or so before the election, but the man's campaign workers began a campaign of dirty tricks against her.

The man won the nomination, but—partly because many people were turned off by his tactics against the woman—he lost the election.

Several years later, the woman won her party's nomination to another office. One day, her former opponent called her campaign office to offer his support. The woman's advisers and campaign workers, remembering what the man had done to her in the primary election years before, wanted to reject his offer.

The candidate, however, was more tolerant of the political game. She chastised her supporters. "I'm in this race to win," she said. "It's better to have him on our side."

The woman won the election. Then she turned around and offered her former nemesis a position in her administration.

Many of her supporters thought her foolish, but the man did an excellent job for many years and became one of the woman's most loyal aides.

(MD)

The Right (of) Way

"There will be weeping and gnashing of teeth when you see Abraham and Isaac and Jacob and all the prophets in the kingdom of God, and you yourselves thrown out. Then people will come from east and west, from north and south, and will eat in the kingdom of God. Indeed, some are last who will be first, and some are first who will be last."

Luke 13:28-30

Once upon a time, there was a man who prided himself on his abilities as a driver. He wouldn't let his wife drive when he was in the car. Ever. Nor would he let their one teenager drive, even though he was old enough and had his license. They were simply not competent enough, careful enough, responsible enough, the father thought. Which is to say they were not as competent, careful, and responsible as he was, or thought he was.

Moreover, as he drove, the man always favored his family with a running commentary on the mistakes of other drivers. The wife and son, naturally, had long ago learned how to tune out these commentaries.

Well, one day when the family was on vacation, they went for some ice cream. When they were backing out of their parking place—and it was a very crowded parking lot—the man didn't see a car that was coming behind him and plowed right into it! The other car had the right of way, and the daddy was furious, especially because he knew it was his fault. He jumped out of the car and cursed the teenage boy who was the driver of the other car.

All the kid could say was, "You wrecked my graduation present."

"He had the right of way," the wife said to her husband. But the man wouldn't apologize, even though everyone knew he was wrong.

But, like God does to us, the kid forgave him anyway.

(AG)

The Sitter Sisters

"A man had two sons; he went to the first and said, 'Son, go and work in the vineyard today.' He answered, 'I will not'; but later he changed his mind and went. The father went to the second and said the same; and he answered, "I go, sir'; but he did not go. Which of the two did the will of his father?"

Matthew 21:28-31

Once upon a time, not so very long ago, there were two sisters who were the neighborhood baby sitters. One evening a new couple on the block hired one sister to baby-sit for their children. When they returned home, the house was a mess, the sitter was half asleep on the couch, and it was obvious that the children had not followed their routine of washing up and brushing their teeth.

The next morning, the children were excited. They told their parents how the sitter had played with them and told them wonderful stories and run races with them and helped them say their prayers before they went to sleep. Still, the parents decided they would not use a sitter who left such a mess again.

The next time they went out, they hired the other sister. When they returned home this time, the house was neat and orderly, the children asleep, the baby sitter at the table studying. She reported that the children had been angels and there were no problems. The parents were very pleased with her and gave the girl an extra tip.

The next morning, the children complained. The sitter had yelled at them, used swear words, made them go to bed early, and then went outside and smoked and talked with some of her friends.

Which of the two sitters would you use?

(MD)

The Speculators

> Then Jesus said to the chief priests, the officers of the temple police, and the elders who had come for him, "Have you come out with swords and clubs as if I were a bandit? When I was with you day after day in the temple, you did not lay hands on me. But this is your hour, and the power of darkness!"
>
> *Luke 22:52-53*

Once there was a woman stockbroker who presided over a very successful mutual fund. It was a highly speculative fund and identified as such. It made tons of money, gaining twice as much as the Dow average during its first year.

The woman was a hero to everyone except her rivals in her own company. Many of her investors were ecstatic about her skills as the fund manager.

Then a financial crisis came along and battered everyone in the stock market, but especially those who owned speculative funds. Much, but not all, of the profit the woman had built up for her clients was wiped out.

She began to receive hate mail, especially

hate e-mail (which tends to be the nastiest of all), vicious phone calls, and even threats on her life. Her rivals in the company chortled with glee.

As suddenly as it started, however, the decline stopped, the market stabilized, and then the fund began to climb again. Many of the woman's investors ignored its revival and return to its former success, however.

"You let us down," they berated her.

"Investment is for the long term," the woman pleaded with them.

That argument did not satisfy those who wanted immediate gains without any risk of loss. That apparently was what "speculative" meant to them.

Jesus knew all about these kinds of people.

(AG)

The Spirit of Christmas

> The angel said to them, "Do not be afraid, for see—I am bringing you good news of great joy for all the people: to you is born this day in the city of David a Savior, who is the Messiah, the Lord."
>
> *Luke 2:10-11*

Once upon a time, not too long ago, there were four bachelor commodity brokers who spent most of their free time together. Without even thinking twice about it, they took their dates to the most expensive restaurants, smoked the best cigars, wore the trendiest watches, and thoroughly enjoyed the good life. They did these things not to be showy but because they could afford it. And it seemed that everyone they worked with did the same thing.

One Christmas Eve, their workday over early, the quartet of friends did the same thing they did at the end of every workday—they went bar hopping. But things downtown were pretty dead. Eventually they found themselves walking past the cathedral as people were hurrying in to one of the Christmas Eve masses, greeting one another cheerily. This made them uneasy. None of them ever spent much time in church and they certainly had no plans to attend a Christmas service.

When they came to the convenience store just north of the church, one of them decided he wanted some gum. He entered the store to find the owner berating a young woman of about seventeen, who was in tears. He was able to ascertain that she was trying to buy a cheap Christmas toy for her daughter but did not have enough money to pay the tax on the item. The clerk was adamant. She must pay the tax. As she went to leave the store, the broker touched her arm and said, "I think you dropped this money I found just outside the door." He handed her two twenty-dollar bills.

The woman eyed him warily until he said, "I think your daughter will be happy with Santa's gift." He tucked the money into her purse and rapidly left the store without his gum. He told his buddies the story and then said that he thought maybe he'd go back to the cathedral since there wasn't anything else to do.

They all went with him.

(MD)

The Terrible Twins

"While he was still far off, his father saw (his son) and was filled with compassion; he ran and put his arms around him and kissed him. Then the son said to him, 'Father, I have sinned against heaven and before you; I am no longer worthy to be called your son.' But the father said to his slaves, 'Quickly, bring out a robe—the best one—and put it on him; put a ring on his finger and sandals on his feet. And get the fatted calf and kill it, and let us eat and celebrate; for this son of mine was dead and is alive again; he was lost and is found!' And they began to celebrate."

Luke 15:20-24

Once upon a time, there was a mother who had twins when her next oldest was a senior in high school. The woman was surprised but happy, for she loved all her children.

The twins were so cute and so lively that she figured they'd keep her young. Alas for her, as they grew up the twins were monsters! They fought with each other; they fought with other children. They lied; they stole; they broke things deliberately. Whenever the two of them outnumbered another child, they beat up on that child and then told their mother that the other kid had started the fight. They never studied in school. They tormented all their teachers. They were mean and nasty to their parents and to every other adult they encountered, including their older brothers and sisters. The twins started drinking in sixth grade and were smoking pot in eighth grade.

The mother did her best, but she simply could not control her two adorable but vicious little hellions. Neither could anyone else.

The summer they were fourteen, they stole their mother's car and totaled it. They ended up in the hospital where they made life miserable for the nurses and the doctors. The parish priest even suggested to the mother that she send them off to boarding school. (He thought they should go to a place that had barbed wire and cut glass on the tops of the walls.)

"No," the mother said, "I would miss them too much if they weren't home with the rest of us. I'm their mother, and I love them."

And that's exactly the way it is with God and us.

(AG)

The Too-Busy Samaritan

"Do not be afraid, little flock, for it is your
Father's good pleasure to give you the kingdom. Sell your possessions, and give alms.
Make purses for yourselves that do not wear
out, an unfailing treasure in heaven, where
no thief comes near and no moth destroys.
For where your treasure is, there your heart
will be also."

Luke 12:32-34

Once a family was driving home from a summer
vacation. It had been a good vacation and everyone
was happy about it, including the daddy, who had a
reputation of being something of an impatient man.

The vacation was now over, however, and it
was time to get back to the real world. To do this
with the greatest amount of efficiency—the daddy
always prized efficiency—the family had to leave
the vacation house at noon on Sunday to beat the
late-afternoon traffic.

Well, mommies and kids being what they
are, they had not even begun to load the car at
noon. Nor at 1:00. Nor even at 1:30. Finally, they hit
the highway at 1:45, right on the cusp of Sunday
traffic. With a little bit of luck, they would miss the

worst of it, though there would be delays at the tollgates.

They had driven about a half mile down the road when they saw one of those little cars that parents give their kids for graduation pulled over at the side of the road with a flat tire.

"Melissa has a flat tire," one of the kids shouted. (Melissa was a teenager who baby-sat for the family at their summer home.)

"We should stop and help her," the mommy said. (Mommies are always saying things like that.)

"We haven't got time," the Daddy said as he drove on. "We have to beat the traffic. Someone else will surely help her."

The car was very silent the rest of the way home.

(AG)

The Treasure

> "The kingdom of heaven is like treasure hidden in a field, which someone found and hid; then in his joy he goes and sells all that he has and buys that field."
>
> *Matthew 13:44*

According to a Jewish folk tale, a poor beggar lived in a run-down house in the city of Krakow. He was so poor that he usually went without fuel for his stove. This beggar had a recurring dream about a treasure in a box near a bridge in the city of Prague. The dream was so real that he decided he must go and look for the treasure.

The man walked the long journey to Prague and found the bridge of his dream, but it was in the Gentile section of the city. Before he had a chance to search for the treasure, he was stopped and questioned. The police laughed at his story. How stupid he was to believe in a dream!

One of the officers said that he, too, had been having a dream about a treasure hidden under a useless stove in the kitchen of a beggar's hovel in the city of Krakow. He, however, was not foolish enough to waste his time and make the journey to Krakow just because of a dream.

When the officers tired of making fun of the beggar, they sent him on his way, telling him to go home, work hard, and forget about dreams. The man hurried home, making the return journey in much less time than it had taken him to get to Prague. He immediately rushed to the stove in his kitchen. Underneath it he found a treasure large enough to make him a wealthy man for the many, many remaining years of his life.

(MD)

The Unforgiving Congregation

> (Jesus) breathed on them and said to them, "Receive the Holy Spirit. If you forgive the sins of any, they are forgiven them; if you retain the sins of any, they are retained."
>
> *John 20:22-23*

Once upon a time, long ago and far away, an unmarried woman gave birth to a son. The laws of her church required that she repent of her sin and identify the father of her child. When she refused to name the man, the church community voted to banish her from their midst. The woman and her son continued to live in the village, but when her son grew to adulthood, he left the town forever.

One day, however, his mother, lonely and eager to make her peace with God, went to the new pastor of the church and asked forgiveness. She told him she had never wanted to name the father of her child because it would have caused great sorrow for that married man's family and forced him to give up his prominent position in the community. And even though the man had died, she would still not identify him. The pastor forgave her sin and promised to ask the church community to welcome her back. At the next gathering of the congregation, the pastor presented her case to the members and asked for a vote for her readmission to the congregation. The members, though, cast a unanimous vote against her.

At the end of the service, the pastor stood and announced that this would be the congregation's last meeting. The church would be closing its doors forever. Since the members were unwilling to be witnesses to Jesus' admonition to "judge not and you will not be judged, " the community was no longer a sign of God's Spirit in their world.

The next day, several members of the congregation approached the pastor and asked if he would assemble the people one more time the next Sunday for another vote on the repentant woman's fate. They then spent the remainder of the week encouraging their fellow members to see what the pastor was trying to tell them about themselves as a community. The second vote was unanimous for accepting the woman back into the congregation.

The Spirit of God is a constant challenge to all believers.

(MD)

The Unquenchable Thirst

Jesus said to her, "Everyone who drinks of this water will be thirsty again, but those who drink of the water that I will give them will never be thirsty. The water that I will give will become in them a spring of water gushing up to eternal life." The woman said to him, "Sir, give me this water, so that I may never be thirsty or have to keep coming here to draw water."

John 4:13-15

Once upon a time, there was a man who was a prisoner of war. The camp in which he was held was a cruel, harsh place and the guards were brutal. Many men died.

The soldier was sick often and hungry always. Once he almost died of thirst. But his worst suffering was the separation from his home and family and his fear that he would never see them again.

Every day, the man prayed that he might live long enough to go home and quench his thirst for his family. After many years, the war was finally over and the solider went home.

He was deliriously happy to be reunited with his wife and children and they with him. But as time

went on it seemed to him that they didn't understand all that he had suffered, and the terrible thirst
he had experienced for their love was never totally
quenched.

"You don't understand," he often told his
family. "You just don't understand what it was like."

Finally his teenage daughter said to him,
"Daddy, you don't understand what it was like for
us."

(AG)

The Wedding Dress

"I give you a new commandment, that you love
one another. Just as I have loved you, you
also should love one another."

John 13:34

Once upon a time, not too very long ago, there
was a mother who sewed many of her daughters'
clothes. This mom had learned the art of sewing
from her own mom, who in turn had learned it from
her mom.

This mom made holiday dresses, party
dresses, and finally prom dresses for her five
daughters. When the first of the daughters to marry
started looking through bride's magazines, she
asked her mom if she might be able to make a
wedding dress.

Responding to the challenge, the mom spent
many hours over the next five months sewing
pearls and sequins on lace that was then attached
to the dress. As she sewed, the mom found herself
feeling very close to her deceased mother. She
remembered the many dresses her mother had
made for her over the years, and how proud she

always felt in her "originals."

And although her grandmother had died some seventy years before, the mom also began feeling connected to her. Often, as she sat by herself in the evenings, sewing the small beads, she sensed the presence of these two women and experienced a feeling of being loved by both of them.

The woman hoped that her daughter would feel that the love of her mother, her grandmother, and her great-grandmother was sewn into her wedding dress.

And that this memory would help her pass that same love on to the next generation.

(MD)

The Wedding of the Year

> As Jesus passed along the Sea of Galilee, he saw Simon and his brother Andrew casting a net into the sea—for they were fishermen. And Jesus said to them, "Follow me and I will make you fish for people." And immediately they left their nets and followed him. As he went a little farther, he saw James son of Zebedee and his brother John, who were in their boat mending the nets. Immediately he called them; and they left their father Zebedee in the boat with the hired men, and followed him.
>
> *Mark 1:16-20*

When Bill and Mary, two promising young physicians, announced their engagement, everyone began to talk about what a gala their wedding would be.

Bill's dad was a prominent doctor in the city, and many of the political, social, religious, and cultural leaders of the community were his patients.

Mary's mom was CEO of the largest company in the city, and she and her husband were very active in all the city's major activities.

Both sets of parents began to plan the wedding: Bill and Mary would be married by the bishop in the cathedral, with a reception afterward at the swankiest hotel in town that would be the event of the year.

Imagine the parents' surprise when, two weeks after their engagement, the young couple announced that they had been invited by a senior doctor at the hospital to join her on a yearlong project treating malaria patients in Africa. They would need to leave in less than a month, and they decided that they would have a small wedding ceremony the following Saturday in the hospital chapel with the hospital chaplain officiating.

Sometimes following Jesus doesn't happen according to the social calendar.

(MD)

The Woman Who Missed the Surprises

> Jesus replied, "A man was going down from Jerusalem to Jericho, and fell into the hands of robbers, who stripped him, beat him, and went away, leaving him half dead. Now by chance a priest was going down that road; and when he saw him, he passed by on the other side. So likewise a Levite, when he came to the place and saw him, passed by on the other side. But a Samaritan while traveling came near him; and when he saw him, he was moved with pity."
>
> *Luke 10:30-33*

Once upon a time, a certain woman went on a vacation with her husband and three children. She didn't want to go, because she had been on vacations with her family before and knew that they just meant more work for her.

A vacation was like being home, the woman thought, only you had your husband and your kids under your feet all the time—not just part of the day. Moreover, they make more demands on you than usual as they try to adjust to a strange place.

This is fun? Give me a break, she decided.

However, the woman was overruled, especially by her children. So they went on a vacation. It was even worse than before. The weather was hot and humid every day for two weeks—except for two evening thunderstorms that knocked out both the television and the refrigerator. The kids missed their friends. Her husband was on the phone to his office every day.

Relax? You gotta be kidding, the woman thought.

So she didn't notice how helpful the rest of the family was, how easily her kids made friends, how beautiful were the water and the sky and the sunsets, how warm the water was for swimming, how nice her husband was when he wasn't on the phone, how good the meals were at the local restaurants, how friendly the neighbors were, how much fun they had. Because she was judging by previous vacations, she was not open to being surprised.

So when the surprises came, she missed them.

(AG)

Three Blind Mothers

> Now the eleven disciples went to Galilee, to the mountain to which Jesus had directed them. When they saw him, they worshiped him; but some doubted.
>
> *Matthew 28:16-17*

A group of three young mothers who lived on the same street agreed to pool their time and resources so that they could help one another take care of their kids and at the same time provide one another with a little free time.

The co-op worked fine. The kids liked it, the fathers liked it (anything to escape from the demands of child-rearing), and, most importantly, the women liked it. They discovered in practice what they had heard so often in theory: it's easier to do things as members of a community than as isolated individuals.

The women bragged to their friends on other streets about how well their little community worked and how everyone should try to imitate them. But then one of the three women began to tally up the hours she gave to the community effort and concluded that she was giving more time than the other two. Those two added up their own times and concluded just the opposite. Indeed they accused the first woman of making up her numbers so she could escape her fair share.

Since they had all studied economics in college, the women began to shout "free rider" at one another. Soon they were not speaking at all. Their community collapsed under the pressures of success, resentment, and envy—in that order.

"See, we told you so," said the neighbors on other streets.

None of the three could ever see what went wrong.

(AG)

True Hope

> "Understand this: if the owner of the house had known in what part of the night the thief was coming, he would have stayed awake and would not have let his house be broken into. Therefore you also must be ready, for the Son of Man is coming at an unexpected hour."
>
> *Matthew 24:43-44*

Once there was a young woman who was eager to have a baby. One of her friends (to test her) asked, "Why are you and your husband so set on having children? You know that their lives will be filled with suffering and disappointment. You know that they will cause you heartache and pain. You know there will be times when they will hate you and other times that you will be very angry at them. You know there will be terrible pain often in their lives. You know that someday you will die and they will suffer your loss. You know that they will die too, perhaps horribly, perhaps even before you. It doesn't make any sense at all to have children, does it?"

The future mother replied, "Even if everything goes badly eventually, it is better to have a chance to live, to love, to give, to receive, to believe. When our children come, I will tell them how precious life is and how much they should take from it—which means how much they must also give to it. Above all, I will tell them that it is necessary to hope for their children, just as I hoped for them."

"Hope that they will not suffer and die?" the friend asked.

"No, hope that they will live with enthusiasm and love," the woman replied. "If they live that way, love never ends."

"You have spoken well," her friend said.

(AG)

Vacation Revisited

> Then Jesus gave a loud cry and breathed his last. And the curtain of the temple was torn in two, from top to bottom. Now when the centurion, who stood facing him, saw that in this way he breathed his last, he said, "Truly this man was God's Son!"
>
> *Mark 15:37-39*

Once upon a time, two young people were planning a summer trip to Europe. For months they talked about almost nothing else. They read all the books, they studied all the maps, they bought the right clothes and the right luggage so they could travel light.

When the day of their trip dawned, they were the happiest young persons in the world. The flight over was rough. They both had motion sickness. They stumbled around for a couple of days with jet lag. The immigration and customs inspectors gave them a hard time. Their reservations had been lost. They had a hard time finding an ATM that would take their credit cards. The young people their own age all hated Americans. They both came down with some kind of stomach flu. It rained hard every day.

No one told us, they complained, that traveling required patience and sacrifice. Then they began to fight with each other. They hardly spoke for the last week of the trip. Their month-long trip was, from beginning to end, a disaster.

Finally, the duo came home. The skyline of their city looked like the garden of paradise. They rejoiced that they were back home and that they were Americans.

Yet they told everyone about how wonderful the trip was and how much they had enjoyed all the good times they had together. Then they began to plan their trip for the following summer.

What looks like the end is not always the end.

(AG)

Gospel Index

John

Lectionary Index

Year A

Year B

Year C

Additional Spirituality Resources

The Legend of the Bells and Other Tales
Stories of the Human Spirit
John Shea

Twenty-five of theologian and storyteller John Shea's favorite stories, with the author's reflections on what each story is about and how it can be a window into the world of spirit. (190-page paperback, $12.95)

Grace Is Everywhere
Reflections of an Aspiring Monk
James Stephen Behrens, O.C.S.O.
Foreword by Dolores Leckey
Afterword by Joan Chittister, O.S.B.

Short vignettes from the author's life at the Monastery of the Holy Spirit in Conyers, Georgia, with reflections on the connection between monastic spirituality and daily life. (160-page paperback, $9.95)

Everyday People, Everyday Grace
Daily Meditations for Busy Christians
George R. Szews

Brief stories of ordinary people experiencing God's grace in their everyday lives, coupled with a scripture quotation for each day of the year. (368-page paperback, $9.95)

A Contemporary Celtic Prayer Book
William John Fitzgerald
Foreword by Joyce Rupp

A prayer book that captures the distinctive flavor and sensibility of traditional Celtic spirituality for today's Christians, featuring both a simplified Liturgy of the Hours and a treasury of Celtic blessings, prayers, and rituals for a variety of occasions. (160-page hardcover, $16.95)

Available from booksellers or call
800-397-2282 in the U.S. or Canada.